TOO CLOSE, NOT CLOSE, SO CLOSE

ABAGAIL THOMAS

TOO CLOSE, NOT CLOSE, SO CLOSE

J. Kenkade Publishing

5920 Highway 5 N. Ste. 7

Bryant, AR 72022

www.jkenkadepublishing.com

Social Media: @jkenkadepublishing

J. Kenkade Publishing is a registered trademark.

PERSONAL BIO

Abagail Thomas is a mother, public speaker, poet, writer, and author of the new novel "Too Close, Not Close, So Close". She speaks on issues about her life with her daughter and living after trauma or through severe life stressors. It is not uncommon for lives to unravel after these experiences and her greatest passion is bringing healing to people who have been through trauma. While no single approach is right for every individual, Abagail works hard to help children, adults and families alike find healthy perceptions of themselves so they can live peaceful, whole, and safe lives.

MAIN CHARACTERS:

Anita,Daughter

Naomi, Mother

SUMMARY:

How A Daughter Can Betray Their Mother

Family Members And Men That Are Narcissistic

How To Overcome Life In All Angles

Naomi had her daughter Anita back in 1994. She made sure Anita had anything she could ever want. Anita was a respectful kid, but when she got pregnant at fifteen, she didn't tell Naomi. By the time Naomi found out, Anita was already four months pregnant. When Naomi found out, there was little she could do, because Anita was already so far along. Naomi cursed to herself, wondering what they were going to do. They didn't have any help from Anita's father. Naomi worried she would have to do everything, as the baby's grandmother. Naomi and Anita went to the doctor and found out she was having a boy. The boy Anita claimed was the father was also there. He was a good young man who took responsibility. He gave his last name to their child. Naomi was so happy for her daughter, but tragically, the boy got shot and died.

Anita was so hurt and angry, wondering why he had to be with God instead of her. At the time, Naomi couldn't give her daughter an answer as to why God took good people. Naomi's grandson was about one or two when that boy died, but Anita found out her son wasn't his child.

Later, Naomi and Anita moved to Tampa to stay with Naomi's aunt on her father's side. Naomi found a place on Conway. The population was mostly Hispanic in that area and things were good for them there. Then, Anita got pregnant again. *DAMN*, Naomi thought, *why now?* Anita was not working at all and they now had a second child to take care of. Naomi got a check every month, but she knew it was not going to last a whole month. Naomi tried to work it out, but she already had to pay full rent. The boyfriend that Anita said was the father of her second child was helping her too. Anita could ask him for anything and it was done. Later in Anita's pregnancy, her boyfriend's mother wanted a DNA test to be done. When Naomi's granddaughter was born, she was so beautiful, but the test proved she wasn't his. Shocked, Naomi asked Anita who the father was. Anita admitted to lying and revealed that the father was a grown man who was a friend of Naomi's brother. Then it was getting difficult, and they had to move again. Anita's father was locked up in prison. He was no help at all, despite still being with Naomi. The father of Anita's baby went to court for custody because he found out he was the baby's father and he wanted children. Naomi never thought she would be the type of person that would have sex with more than one partner, but with Anita's father still in prison and unwilling to help, she began to resent him. Naomi said she hated him for that, but he still wanted letters from her. Naomi agreed but told him he needed to talk to Anita before she got pregnant because it's different when a father talks to his kids than when a mother does. For example, when Naomi talked to Anita about what could happen to her, it made her life feel worse. But when Anita talked to her father and he started writing to her, Naomi was so happy because it made Anita happy! Anita started writing him and felt listened to. But then, he stopped writing to her and just wrote to Naomi. He sent her a picture of another woman, telling her that if she wanted him, she should not send it back. Naomi sent the picture back to him with no problem, but asked if he truly didn't want to at least talk to his daughter. He didn't want the responsibility. When her father stopped writing letters, it caused Anita to hurt badly.

Years went by, but eventually, Naomi and Anita got into it and Naomi showed her the letter that he wrote about Anita. It was probably wrong, but she needed to know. Naomi was there for her daughter on days like Christmas, but asked her daughter, "Do you think he did anything?" and told her, "Hell no." Naomi felt bad about it for years.

When Anita had her second child, she found out who the father was, and Naomi and the family moved to the other side of Tampa. Naomi demanded Anita tell her who the baby's father was. Naomi stayed in the same apartment that Anita and her children lived in. Naomi finally met the father. They talked and he said that he would be there for her, but he was really no help.

When Anita turned eighteen, Naomi let her stay a little longer. But when Anita started bringing men into the house, it began to get out of hand. One night, Naomi had to whoop that ass because she was really out the door, but she had come back. Naomi missed her while she was gone. Anita got back on track, even going back to school while Naomi watched her kids for her. One day, just the two of them went shopping. They each bought the same kind of shirt and though

Naomi forgot what they said, she knew she had to be careful with what she represented. Anita went to school the next day and while she was at the bus stop, a car ran over her. They had to use a crank because she was underneath the car. At the time, Naomi was with her aunt on her father's side. When Naomi got the phone call, she went straight to the hospital. When she got there, a doctor told Naomi to wait in a room. Naomi's aunt told her that they did the same thing to her when her son died. Naomi's nerves were shot. The preacher approached her and asked Naomi how she wanted things done. When the doctor came and told Naomi that she could see Anita, Naomi's aunt had to drag her by her arms and legs. Naomi entered the room and started crying. When she looked at Anita, her daughter had tubes in her nose and throat. Her ribs were broken, and they had to cut off one of her breasts and take skin off to cover other skin that had been damaged. One leg was completely paralyzed. Naomi asked the doctor if Anita would ever be able to walk again. The doctor said he didn't know, but right now she could not. "Oh my god," Naomi exclaimed. Anita woke up and Naomi told her aunt she would be staying at the hospital. Naomi was just so glad Anita was alive. Next thing you know, Naomi was in bed beside her daughter and told

Anita that she had a seizure. Anita said she couldn't get up and Naomi told her she was sorry because she knew Anita didn't need that. Anita was in pain, but she told Naomi not to spend the night. Because Anita couldn't bend to ring the bell, Anita's son and Naomi's brothers came to stay with her. Naomi just came to check up on Anita and pray while she was sleeping. Anita started doing a little better, so the doctor sent her home, and they gave her a wheelchair. Naomi knew this was going to be a big change and accepted it. As the months went by, Anita started physical therapy and she began to walk again. She was still living with Naomi, and she was behind on rent. Naomi was dating the uncle of Anita's baby daddy, and he suggested they move into a three-bedroom house he found. Naomi was stressed about how she was going to get the money for this. But one day, Anita scratched a lottery ticket, and it was enough to stay at their apartment or find a new place so Naomi went for a house. They settled there and a year later, Naomi was pregnant. Then Anita got pregnant too. (Thankfully, not by the same man!) Naomi was shocked. She had another son, who t was seventeen and left to be with his father whom he loved *so much* in Tampa. Naomi and the baby's father had a plan because he said that was the only way he would take care of his son. Naomi wanted her son to learn Creole in order to allow him to know his father's side. Naomi already had two grandkids from Anita, and Anita had another baby daddy that was there until she got pregnant. After that, they only saw him once in a blue moon. Naomi told Anita she was blessed because after the accident, the doctor told Anita she couldn't have more children. Anita and Naomi talked about everything.

While Naomi and Anita were going through everything, Naomi's aunt sat watching. Anita kicked her out because Naomi's aunt planned all along to get the room to herself. The aunt told Anita to go get a Brillo Pad and bring Naomi a '*sack of white girl*'. Anita was shocked because she didn't know her until she was eighteen, unlike Naomi. Naomi went to Anita's room. Anita talked about how Naomi wasn't there when Naomi's stepdad tried to touch her. Naomi told him when she used to take Anita to her mother's house not to touch Anita or she would kill him. But because she said this in front of Anita, Anita was scared to tell her what happened because she did not want Naomi go to jail. When she told her mother, she began crying and yelling, and Naomi begged to know why Anita didn't tell her. Anita started fighting with Naomi and all the while, Naomi's aunt looked on with a smile. Naomi yelled at Anita to look at her because she was clearly trying to break them up. Once Anita saw that, then she and Naomi turned around and went off on the aunt. She did all that to try to kick Naomi out and take her place. They had to call the police to remove her.

Naomi started staying with her friend. Anita always wanted to stay with Naomi because she knew Naomi had seizures and Anita wanted to be around to help. But Naomi always told her to live her life and not to forget she had a babysitter. Naomi told her grandmother what she had been going through, but she just told everybody else what the doctors said. It was nothing like talking to great-grandma, who listened -like a counselor. Naomi didn't stop talking about anything; she was not looking for pity, she just needed advice.

The fourth and last baby daddy got into an argument with her that started when she was sleeping on the long couch with their son. This time, Naomi didn't have anywhere to go. They had already been e evicted once, so they stay were staying with his mom at her house. His mom came into the room talking, so Naomi tried to be respectful by not fighting in her house. Naomi was in the kitchen when her baby's father demanded that she get out his mother's house. He hit Naomi in the face and they started to struggle violently. She looked toward his mom's door to see if she would come out, but she didn't. He started pulling Naomi's hair and he forced her straight to the floor, dragging her across it. His sister entered, but she walked right over Naomi, went into the same room his mom was in, and closed the door. He threw Naomi's clothes out, but she yelled and pleaded with him to at least let their son stay, so he did. She sat outside on the porch until 6:00 in the morning. Eventually, his sister came out and told Naomi she could come in and talk to him. Naomi called a friend to pick her up instead. She was so mad that her son had to see what he did. Naomi knew that her baby's father wanted to take their son, so Naomi acted nice until his mom told Naomi she got a phone call that her friend had arrived and was at the circle in front of the apartment. Her friend had shown up with her husband. Naomi quickly grabbed the baby and ran, as the father was right behind her. She quickly placed the baby in the truck and then jumped in herself.

After that, Naomi left Tampa and headed to Georgia. There, she stayed with her grandmother for a while. Then, Anita came and got her own place. It was a nice three-bedroom home. She was living next door to a couple who were both police officers. Anita was doing good and was paying bills on time. She had met this girl that was in her thirties and her sister, who was living with her, didn't want to pay rent. Anita and Naomi told her that her sister wasn't good to her.

Anita got pregnant again. Naomi said to her, "Girl, this is your fourth pregnancy. This guy better work out and be there for you." Naomi realized Anita had found someone a little older to help raise her raise this child. One of the sisters left, but the other one that didn't pay her rent stayed. Anita began having problems with the house, so she had to move into a smaller apartment. It was a duplex that just her immediate family lived in.

In the winter, Naomi was working like a dog. Naomi said Anita had changed. Naomi was staying with Anita and when she came home from work one day, Naomi's paperwork was out in the living room. Naomi asked her, "Why are my important papers out?" She knew her income was disclosed on them. When Anita said her baby's father wanted to see them, Naomi was horrified. This day finally showed Naomi that any trust between her and her daughter was gone, all because a man wanted to know Naomi's business. Naomi found Anita's journal. Naomi had told her when she was young that if she couldn't talk to anybody about her feelings, she should write them down, so Anita wrote some mean stuff. She wrote about how she wanted to be like Naomi. but the tone was jealous. Naomi felt worse than she could describe. She had to think over everything again because she had blocked some stuff out of her memory because it was clear her daughter was not well. Naomi didn't say anything about it, she just left it alone.

Instead, Naomi moved out and lived next door for a few months before getting Anita to take her back to Tampa, where her fourth baby's father still lived. Naomi always said she didn't do second chances, but this time she did. When Naomi moved there, he started talking about how he found a three bedroom, but they actually stayed at a hotel. Naomi paid for it, but then he said he was going to pay. Then one day, he left without telling her. The hotel kicked her out and Naomi's son had to go to the restaurant next door. Naomi called her baby's father to see where he was. Then she called her own father to see if he would pick her up. She waited, but when the baby's father got back, Naomi cursed him out and they were removed from the hotel lobby too. He found a place to stay with his uncle and his uncle's wife and Naomi and their son had to stay there too. Naomi tried to be humble, but then one day, the baby's father came back with attitude. She was trying not to fight with him, so Naomi went silent. He threw away her seizure pills and told her to have a seizure and die. Then, he removed the air conditioner from the window and pawned it off. She continued giving him the silent treatment. She started reading, then she began to clean up in the kitchen. When he arrived, he approached Naomi and punched her in the face, so they began fighting and she stabbed him with the cake mixer. Naomi didn't know it would hurt him so much. His uncle called the police, who arrived with an ambulance for the baby's father. Naomi was panicked and worried for her baby. The police asked where Naomi wanted her child to go; they could either give custody to the father's uncle or he could be sent to foster care. Naomi had to make the decision to leave her child with his uncle.

She told the police that her baby's father had punched her, but when they shone the light in her face, the police didn't see any evidence of that. They put her in the backseat and Naomi was shocked. Naomi kept thinking to herself that she should have just left once her dad came to get her. At first, Naomi couldn't get anybody to bail her out from jail. She even asked her mom, who was going to give her four hundred dollars, but then she changed her mind and said no because she had to get her niece to bond with her so she could get Naomi's .baby. Eventually, Naomi called a friend to come get her, then she stayed with her aunt for several months before she left to go to a shelter.

Trying to get her life back in order, Naomi left Tampa. She moved back to Georgia to live with her grandma, who started to become a negative person. For example, when Naomi wanted to get her own place, she asked her grandmother to take her around to look at places together. Naomi went to a realtor, even though her grandma told her she probably wouldn't get it. Naomi didn't get the place, and later, when her friend was moving out, but she didn't look out for Naomi at all. Naomi began to feel that her grandmother didn't want her to move out, which was she was being so negative. Naomi had been letting it slide for a long time, but she finally told her the deal. Naomi tried to say it in a nice way, but she still felt bad because her grandmother wasn't like that when she raised her. Naomi's mother wasn't better; she gave Naomi away after her first husband left her. From the age of four until she was a teen, Naomi had been with her grandmother. Naomi wanted to see her mother, so she ran away, but when Naomi got there, her mom was married to her second husband and they were both on drugs. Naomi started drinking beer whenever they left to get it on, but it was okay until her mother's husband snuck back into the room and started touching her. Naomi told her mother, who started arguing with him and then the door slammed shut. Next thing Naomi knew, it was completely silent.

The next day, her mother and her husband seemed good again, so Naomi called her grandmother and told her she was ready to come home. Her grandmother said, "I told you so. Your mom hasn't changed."

Naomi got home and while watching tv, she saw a ten-year-old white boy divorce his parents, so Naomi did the same thing, Hell, both her parents were on drugs, so she got her grandmother to help her. Naomi had been *through* it with her children and on her father's side too. Naomi was fed up, not willing to take any more bull from anyone. b

Naomi lived in her house in Georgia for three years and she stopped talking to her grandmother. Anita moved back into Naomi's house, but Naomi told her that she couldn't keep moving around. "Don't do like I did. You want to do better for you and your children. That's all," Naomi said. So they stayed for just three months, but Anita made sure her children were on the straight and narrow, then got her money from a guy friend. Then, Naomi started going with a friend of her grandchild's father who lived across the street. So they got into a huge fight about it.

Anita entered the house and immediately started questioning Naomi, yelling, "What's going on between you two?" Anita was not okay with that at all. One night, Anita was going off on Naomi, asking her, "Why are you with that dude? Are you going to believe him over me?" She also said that he talked about her baby's father, so the men were talking about each other behind one another's backs. Naomi was in this petty situation all over again. Anita was yelling. They were in the living room, but Naomi told her son not to worry and went to the back room in order to put on her shorts so that she was ready for whatever. Anita came to the door, talking sideways. They started fighting and Naomi's friend tried to pull them apart, but that wasn't going to happen. Don't forget, they were all friends before Naomi came into the picture. The friend left because he couldn't handle it. When it was finished, the police came, Naomi told them she wanted Anita to leave and stay away for a while.

Then Anita called Naomi and they forgave each other, so Anita started coming by again. After that, Naomi started watching Anita's kids again because she wanted her grandkids to be stable. Anita was just smoking weed but later on, she started doing molly at the same time. But she respected Naomi's rules by not doing it in the house. It was going well for about four months, but then Anita started getting mad about everything again. Naomi just couldn't do it again, cursing her out. Naomi wouldn't be tried like this. Naomi had told Anita since she was young that the bible said to honor your mother and father. She told Anita not to shorten her days by disrespecting her. Anita told Naomi she wished that she would have a seizure and die. Anita also said that Naomi was not a good mother and slow like her own mother. But Naomi always encouraged her daughter. -She didn't want to treat her daughter like the girl from the movie *Precious*. Naomi did what she could with her. Everybody was always asking why she let Anita treat her like that. They even told her not to let Anita in the house, but Anita was her child, and Naomi couldn't help but miss just talking with her about life. Naomi did all that even when she was angry with Anita, and they still lived in same house. They had fought about four times in Anita's life and Naomi was tired. Her body started having more seizures and Naomi didn't know why she was having so many. She was working seven days a week. not getting her rest because she then had to watch her kids. She was getting rest when she could, but it wasn't enough.

When it was just her and her son, there was no drama. Naomi got a call from her brother and he wanted to move in with her, along with his baby's mother. Her brother was in his twenties and Naomi hadn't spent time with him at all. She only saw him once in a blue moon. He also brought his son too. Naomi fixed up the room for them because she was ready to spend time with her brother and his son. He quickly got a job to support his family. While he was at work, Naomi was with his baby's mother and their son, chilling together and talking about him and how they were always arguing. But Naomi could see that she was a strong woman. Her brother left the girl and his son and went to live with his other baby mama that came to get him. Anita must have told him Naomi was mad at him because his baby's mother called her mom to come pick her up. Naomi was angrier than *she* was.

They were sitting on the porch and Naomi saw Anita and her brother walking over from down the street and Naomi went off on them. The baby's mother was trying to calm Naomi down and she gave his stuff to him. He couldn't come up or into the house, he was just allowed on the driveway. He had never seen Naomi mad at him at all, so he was scared to get his stuff. Anita helped him, and they walked down the street. That night, his baby's mother and his son left, so there was peace again. Anita moved back in unexpectedly. At first, Naomi thought she was just visiting, but then she didn't leave. Things between them seemed okay at that point. Naomi's brother called and asked if he could come over and chill. Naomi said okay, but reminded him she didn't have or smoke weed. He started just sitting in his car and Anita was with him while smoking molly.

Naomi was with someone else, and she was feeling happy to find someone that was not a male prostitute or drug user. Her boyfriend worked and his son worked s too. They helped Naomi see her son because she hadn't seen him in years. She had to go to court for custody so she could get her son back. At that time, the doctor took her license from her because she was having seizures. Naomi saw that it was good to argue just one time in the early stages of a relationship,

Naomi went to work and it was around 8:00 at night when she came home. Her friend was watching her son, but when she called first, he didn't pick up the phone, so she panicked. When she got to the house and it was dark, she banged on the door. He finally opened the door and he said that he was in the bed asleep and her son was in the other room. She argued with him and she hit him in the face, and he told her he would call the police because he was not going be abused by a woman and he wouldn't hit women, either, so he left. Naomi thought that he was messing with her son, which he wouldn't do, but she was thinking that, even though when they first met, he told her that he didn't mess with kids. She begged him to come back because she was wrong for hitting him and he came back.

Naomi enjoyed his company and his love. He was so respectful. He just made her feel like a queen. He took her and her son to Red Lobster and proposed with a ring. It was so nice that he did that. The last ring she had was one she bought for herself, but that was not the same. They were engaged for real. She found out he was doing molly too. He said he just drank beer and that he didn't smoke weed, but Naomi did. He played this role for several months before it came out. Boy, people need to stop playing. The truth will come out. Naomi had already smoked weed with his son and he was grown, but he was like a son to her. One day, Naomi's fiancé was chilling in his man-cave and Anita and their friends were chilling in there. Naomi didn't have a problem with it at first, but then she showed up. She was feeling left out, but at first, she let it go and accepted it. Then, outside, Naomi told him that she said from day one that she couldn't be around drugs besides weed, which some say is not a drug, but rather, a plant. Her fiancé did molly and it became the weekend thing. He had his molly and cocaine powder and now it was every weekend. Anita would come over with her boyfriend on those weekends. He was a nice dude and he worked. They were together for a while and now he was on molly with her.

Naomi and her fiancé went out and she left her card in her drawer and Anita stole her money. When Naomi got home, she went to check how much she had on the card, not knowing that Anita took it because she had never stooped to this level with her. Naomi called Anita into the room asked her if she took the money. Anita promised she would pay her back, but Naomi just shook her head because she was stealing from her own mother. Naomi's fiancé's baby mama came over to bring his children to the house. She respected Naomi, but she always got it in his head that he wouldn't be able to see the kids and that's how things had been throughout every relationship that he'd been in. She messed things up for him, but he always messed up by allowing her to do that because everyone has a choice. He told Naomi when they first met how he left her for doing that and one day her own mother sent him photos of her private area and had sex with him. Naomi said, "Wow!" and asked him if he really did that. He responded, "I did because she had sex with my homeboy." That was why he did it. Naomi wondered to herself what she had gotten herself into. All Naomi told him was that she was gay before. Could she really marry this man? Still, she tried to make it work. Later, his own baby mama tried to pick a fight. She called his mother just to start a mess and his mother told Naomi what she said. One day, she came over to Naomi's house to drop the kids off. When she picked her kids up, she was arguing with him, and she put Naomi in the middle of it, so Naomi had to grin and bear it. His baby mama was going off, but eventually Naomi snapped back because she saw the kids. She just told him that he better get his ex out of there because she didn't want to drag her in front of the kids. She left. Naomi went into the house and he said that she had claws in him.

It was the end of February. They were laying down in bed, having sex, but when all that was over, Naomi got in the shower and cried, asking herself, "Why are you settling for this dude? Do you not know what you are worth? He is not the one."

Naomi got a phone call from her uncle, who said someone had been looking for her. It was Naomi's sister, though they weren't related by blood. Naomi had known her since they were little. Naomi was happy. Her uncle gave her the number, so she called, and they talked about old times and what Naomi was going through with her relationship. Naomi introduced her fiancé to her sister and they talked. But Naomi's fiancé got distant, and every time she called, he asked her if she was gay. That question popped up because she told him in the beginning of their relationship that she used to be gay, so later on, he thought she might still be gay. He was also still doing molly and he started bringing his coworker over and they would do it outside. Naomi and her fiancé got into an argument;

he told Naomi that he was leaving and that he wasn't playing. He wanted to sleep with her before he left, but Naomi did not want that. He left. It was over.

Naomi looked at the relationship from all angles. Her sister said she should move up to where she was and live with her. Naomi said that she couldn't because she had to go to court to get her son, but her son told her that he just wanted to spend the summer time with her. She fought for her son for the longest time; her ex-fiancé even tried to help her. Naomi started feeling depressed and began doing drugs again. Anita got the drugs for her.

Naomi's seizures started to increase, all back-to-back. Naomi had a bad one when she was in bed asleep. The sheet was around her neck, so Anita's friend came out to help Naomi. He reminded Naomi that Anita stole the money, and told her he was the one that was helping Naomi, not Anita. He told Naomi that Anita didn't want to help. Naomi just cried. Naomi said Anita used to be there for her. Naomi guessed Anita was tired of saving her, but she didn't know for sure. She called her sister to pick her up and her sister said that she was on the way with her crew. While she was waiting, Naomi got messed up on drugs.

Naomi then thought to herself that she had come too far to go backwards. She told Anita she could take over the four-bedroom house because she had the kids and Anita agreed.

Naomi went further on her journey north. Naomi was staying with her sister. She couldn't find a place because that was when the coronavirus first started. They had a curfew and everything was going down, but Naomi was checking in with Anita every month. Before Naomi left, Anita told Naomi's sister that Naomi was an evil person again, but she tried to love Anita from a distance. In August, Anita called Naomi and asked for her Facebook account. Naomi asked her why, but Anita got mad and hung up on her.

It was September. Naomi's money wasn't on her card, so she called to see what was going on. The lady told Naomi that her bank account was switched over to another account and she was not supposed to give out that information. Naomi had to think. Anita called her in July, and she also moved out of the house. She told Naomi that her mail came to her new address. Little did she know, Naomi already changed her address. Naomi knew Anita had opened her mail. She just didn't understand; when Anita lived with her, she always paid her rent. Naomi's sister told her that she was so sorry that she was going through that. Naomi had to cancel everything. Naomi had not talked to Anita since. It was like she didn't want to be saved. Naomi had to let her go and forgive her. Anita still tried her, but it didn't work. Naomi prayed that one day, she would get better and not think of Naomi as a bad person. Naomi wished all the best for her daughter and grandkids. She guessed she would see them when they got older. Naomi's son, who was the second oldest, kept telling Naomi what Anita was doing. Naomi knew that her son was still trying to keep the peace between them. It was hard, but Naomi learned that her own family members can be narcissists. She realized that people should find comprises and have respect for one another.

Respect needs to go both ways in a relationship, but we can't help everyone. Only the ones that *want* healthy relationships with family or friends can be helped. If you can't get there with someone, let it go, live your life, go for your dreams, and become who God wants you to be. That's your gift that's inside of you.

A sign that you are dealing with a narcissist is that these individuals will promise that they will someday return to you. You become trauma bonded and gain false hope. It's not a friendship; rather, it's a form of supply for them. If they backstab close friends, they will do the same to you. They have no need for you. They want someone to take care of them. Once they find that, they will hide. They rely on media for external gratification. They have Facebook accounts that are set up to only be accessible to r close friends. This is for their supply. They will hide everything from you and the people they love and when you enter a relationship with them, they try to control the status. They own you. They cheat on their partners and hide it, hoping the partner will find out on their own. Usually the partner and soon-to-be ex will be friends. You give them trust, love, and value, but they give you low self-esteem, guilt, and shame. Sometimes these tactics are done subconsciously. If they leave you, they will try to get back together with you by saying that they will become perfect. They will leave you in the end, hoping you'll still be friends with them or someone in your mutual circle. This is when they reveal their partner. You can lash out, but if you do, they will act like you're the one who caused them pain. They will not take responsibility for any of their actions. You'll be wrong and the narcissist will be right. They will get revenge. Everything they tell you will be a lie.

You have to remind yourself that they don't love you; you're not even friends. Look at their friends. Have you ever wondered why you never met some of them? It's because they are either dating them or using them. They will never want to meet your friends either, even though you will have to meet theirs. They will try to make you bond with their friends so they can keep tabs on you. They look at your social media. They hate seeing others happy. They compare themselves to others.

One thing it's going to be important to know is who you are and what you want to do in life. Sometimes we meet these people in order to learn narcissists are puzzling, contradictory creatures. One contradiction is that they can be nice and kind, yet cruel and toxic. It will make you wonder if the nice and kind them is the fake one.

One thing that makes narcissists miserable being ignored. Narcissists act like victims, going on with their lives and appearing happy. There are no specific lists or a certain number of signs, but you'll notice if you stop calling or texting them, not saying a word, they will text you to see if they can still get their supply from you. Why do narcissists lie? The reason is that they're trying to confuse you, which means ultimately there is no excuse for lying to you. A narcissist with their mask on will successfully fool everyone. They will not leave you confused; Instead, they leave you confident, certain, inspired, and love-bombed. It's the unmasked narcissist who will leave you confused and disregarded once they leave you permanently. Cognitive dissonance is the true state of the narcissist's mind. Do not trust them or give them compassion. That means not believing a word they say or expecting them to do the right thing. You should go with no-contact with them if possible. It's not cowardice; life is just too short to be toyed around with and treated like persona non grata. Don't you have something to do? Don't you have better places to be? You're not even making the narcissist happy. What does a trauma bond with a narcissist look like? It's an emotional experience, usually with a toxic person. It holds you emotionally captive to the narcissist who keeps you hostage, whether that be through physical or emotional abuse. You know the narcissist is deceptive and conniving, but you can't seem to let go. You may be a rational, discerning person who sees through all of the narcissistic games. But evading their attempts to manipulate you won't come easy.

Naomi was dating a younger guy. He was thirty years old and dating three women. One woman was the main woman, with a secured job and that was the woman that he stayed with. Naomi was the fourth woman. They started out as just friends because she knew what he had going on. Then they started going together, but she was still trying to hold back. Then he started coming over to chill and smoke weed after he got off work. They talked. He wanted to get a place together and leave the older white lady. This was not the main lady. Naomi gave him advice; she told him not to let that old lady treat him like he was nothing.

Naomi couldn't live in the house with him. It was getting out of hand. He wanted to have sex with his main girl and Naomi, which she was not okay with. He wanted to video it when they had sex. Naomi told him the video better not get back to the main girl, but it did. She synced their phones and saw the whole video. Naomi was so mad that they stopped talking. Then he got mad and when Naomi called his phone, he put the main girl on the phone to tell Naomi not to call him. Now she knew about Naomi and she already knew where Naomi lived too. But Naomi didn't get into fights with any of his women. After seven days, he called, but she let it ring, so he came over. Naomi didn't answer the door at all. He banged on the window and they argued until he left, but he came back so they could talk. Naomi told him to marry the main girl because she would put up with the other women. Naomi and him argued back and forth. The same day he got married, right afterward, he came by and to Naomi with the ring on. Naomi went off and told him not to come by and that it was over. He just said next time, he wouldn't come over with the ring on. Naomi said she blocked him on everything. She had been through a lot. One thing she disliked with any man was when they fed her this fantasy about their relationship and how it was working. Some people said you had to work at it. She didn't want to be a fool.

She still got the short end of the stick, as she ended up dating a lot of narcissistic men. Naomi went back to her old ways, having sex with a man and paying for his services so that everything happened the way that she wanted it to. Naomi started thinking that it was better if it was just sex, because then she didn't have to go through the heartaches she went through in relationships. Who doesn't want good sex with no drama?

Women try to save men, saying he won't treat them like that, but he will. We mess up by not listening when a man is talking, They do tell us things when we ask questions. For instance, when Naomi met the man that was with multiple women, he was honest and told Naomi he was seeing a few women so that they could take care of him.

Naomi had a few friends too, but she wasn't having sex with them. She talked on the phone with one of her friends. He was having sex to get money. Naomi had noticed that he was different. She knew he had a job because Naomi had been with men who didn't have jobs and they were losers. They wanted her to pay for everything, so she fantasized to herself about how it would feel to not be the main girl and have less responsibility.

He treated Naomi with respect. The main girl always went through hell with her man. Naomi really had to sit back and absorb it because she used to be the main girl and she went through hell. That's why being a side chick was really the fantasy in her mind. The main girls really went through problems, but the side chick was just a sex partner. But it turned out, men came to their side girls with their problems too. The man who was with multiple women claimed was a victim through it all. Even though he had a few women, he still acted like the victim because he was trying to find his mate. That's the story men tell women; he acted like he was in the movie *Coming to America.*,

Naomi asked him, "Do you love me?" and reminded him that they had been together for two years. Naomi asked to see if they needed to go down that road because she was catching feelings and she wanted more. He told her he loved everybody and was just living his life.

When Naomi went out of town, he texted her that he loved her and told her to have fun. But he also told her to come back home and said that he was going to come down there and get her. Naomi learned with her baby's father that you can do wife duties but still be the side girl. She learned she should have listened when he told her he wasn't ready to do the couple thing. He didn't have any money, but he loved her, and that was all he had to give. At that time, love was what she needed, so she said it couldn't be that bad, but the whole two years were worse than she thought. She was scared. She had just gotten out of a relationship, and she didn't need a man, but she learnt with the fourth man that the lord had her be with another narcissist to teach her a lesson. She had to stop assuming things based on her own understanding because when that man told her he was coming to get her, she looked at the text and thought he really loved her, but he didn't. He just wanted to have his cake and eat it too. Men have been doing this for years. They make women think that they're going to get married. Naomi had a dream, and she thought her baby's father was going to be her husband. She was making decisions based off that dream. She told his mom that they were getting married. She was doing too much. Naomi prayed about things and she asked God what she should do. This was the first time she had done this because she had always done what she wanted and went by her own understanding, but she was sick and tired of it. She said she was done and that it took two people to be in a relationship.

If you know better, you won't get hurt again and again and again. Do you want narcissists to keep lying to you, hurting you, and making you feel like less than a woman?

Ever since Naomi had been on this earth, she had seen a woman stay with a man for thirty years and take everything. Her kids got messed with and she got beaten up until she listened to him. He threatened to kill the woman because he didn't want her to be with anyone else.

Naomi was now forty years old. Love was hard. She didn't have any problems except that she did get her feelings hurt sometimes. If she wanted a relationship, then she had to snap back.

When Naomi was in her twenties, she met an older woman. She just wanted to try out being with a lady, and she thought the other woman understood. Naomi was sure it couldn't be worse than being with a man if she didn't think like a man. The lady didn't dress like a man; her clothes were feminine. Naomi was surprised because she thought it would be different, but it was the same with a woman too. Letting things go was the difference. She had let a lot slide her life. Naomi had been through abuse her since she was four years old and people let that slide in her family, so she let the men in her life slide too. She knew at forty-one not to let it slide if a man with a drug or alcohol addiction beat or mentally abused her.

If a man cheats on you or with you and he says he's going to change, don't let that slide because if you do, he will continue to do it when you marry him. A woman should know what she is worth and if a man doesn't want to live by God's love, she needs to let him move on because God will send her the one and she doesn't have to lower her standards. Some say there's not anyone for them. They say it will be a long time before they find someone or that certain people aren't their types. We miss our blessings like that.

Naomi said that because she almost found that relationship. But now, Naomi could focus on herself. Women tell their friends that won't be them, but then they end up in that situation. Naomi did both. Then, after coming to the light, you start asking why you did that for so long. So Naomi asked God to direct her path. She had a relationship with God, but there were some things that she still didn't understand and she always had to encourage herself. Just after her relationship, Naomi learned to pray for others.

Naomi grew up seeing her great-grandma with her husband for years, 'til death did them part.

Friends and family may say you just pick the wrong person, but sometimes you can see what's good in that person when they can't. But if the bad outweighs the good, they've got to go, or you will get drained. You will lose weight and your body will shut down. You know what I'm talking about.

Naomi didn't see it and kept trying her best to make the relationship work and kept praying because she knew God could change things. She looked back over her life. She knew that every man wanted a good woman, but some were not ready, and some were. While she was trying to figure these men out, she was hurting herself. She just needed to let go and let God in.

Remember, you are not what has happened to you; you are what you choose to become. When you stop chasing the wrong things, you give the right things a chance. Don't mistake silence for weakness. Smart woman don't plan big moves out loud. Don't let any man pull you low enough to hate him. Stay away from men who make you feel like you are hard to love. Sometimes the wrong man helps us to find the right man.

If you feel depressed or afraid:

Psalms 34:4; Matthew 28:2; Timothy 1:7; Hebrews 13:5,6.

If you need guidance, read the following: Psalms 32:8.

For Excuses, read the following:

Luke 14:15-24.

For Love:

Luke 10:27; 1 Corinthians 13:3.

If you're a loner and have limitations:

When Naomi first found out that she had epilepsy at age 17, she'd already had a baby at 16. The father was in prison for 25 years, so she was alone and had to take care of her child all by herself. Before that, all of the doctors told her that she couldn't have children and that she would be *Driving Miss Daisy* the rest of her life.

She didn't realize at first that the doctor gave her Dilantin, which had her sleeping all day. It was like she was sleeping her life away, so she told her grandmother that she couldn't live like that. They kept putting her on different drugs, like she was a guinea pig, just to find the right one. She had staring seizures and then start having grand mal seizures. Naomi felt like a prisoner in her own body. Later on, she wanted to work and started at age 20. That's when the doctor got her on track and it was okay for her to work her first job at the Walmart deli. It was going well, so she wanted to get another job as a stocker; she worked until 6:00 in the morning, then took the children to school. She had two children at this time, so in addition, she wanted to get a third job at Pizza Hut on the weekend. One day, she had gotten off work and while in the car, as she was backing out, she felt a seizure coming on, but she couldn't stop it and she backed into a work truck. When the seizure was over, the police and everybody were around her and she asked what happened. The police wrote up a report. Weeks went by, and the man who owned the work truck came to her job to harass her. He said if she didn't pay, they would take her license. They did take it and she had to wait one year to get her license back. She had to stop working three jobs, so she quit Pizza Hut and then only had two jobs. She just couldn't believe that she was going through this. She'd ask, "Why me?" Older people would answer, "Why not you?" She cried, asking her grandma what she did so wrong and why God was doing this to her. She just wanted good in her life.

"I'm going to work and taking care of my kids. Yes, I am doing it in moderation and I'm not always at work," said Naomi, but she started thinking if she just moved to another state, things might be different. She moved to Florida, but when she got there, she was still having seizures and couldn't drive. Six years went by, and she was tired of having walk to work or catch the bus. She kept thinking she was not getting anywhere and she had two kids. She didn't want her kids thinking she couldn't do it. She always asked herself why things were like this. She did have that car accident and could have died. Still, it was hard living in those boundaries. She couldn't work that much but she loved working. She had to learn that she couldn't tell the people in charge of her job that she had seizures because they wouldn't hire her. Finally, she got a place of her own because her aunt told her she didn't need to work and that staying home to raise the kids that was the hardest thing to do. She was still not driving either. How could she cope? She had to drive, so then she learned to tell the doctor that she hadn't had a seizure in a year because that was the only way for her to get her license back. Once she seemed better, then she would get her license back.

Naomi got her own place and lived there with her kids. Everyone was against her, but she got stronger. Then she got a nursing job and took care of the elderly.

She was in the church all of her life and had tried believing in different gods, thinking it would help. But it really depressed her to stay in her room a lot and think that she couldn't do anything. She was a determined person and always wondered what could she could do next.

Naomi started taking EKG and that's when the doctor said they were going by that and they took her license again. She said, "Naomi, you need to move away from Florida."

Naomi had three kids now. The man that she had the third baby with didn't do anything at all. She did everything on her own and couldn't get government assistance. The second baby daddy told the housing authority that she was working, so they had to pay all that money back. First of all, she had to divorce her parents to get where she was and get a job and a car. That man just messed all that up in one day, assuming that she was cheating because she had a man in the car. But she was just giving him a ride to his girl's house. Naomi thought he was bluffing, but before going up to the office, he told her to stop him. She didn't, so he did it. After that, she couldn't get housing or anything from the government. Next, the baby's father also didn't want to help unless the child was with him. She needed help buying his clothes for school. The father already took her child two years ago, so she had to find him. She let her son go with his father, but she did have other kids that she had to support, so she left town and went to another state to settle the matter. But it had been four years; the baby daddy didn't want to give the child up and he had a lady helping him raise their child, so she didn't want to give him up either. Naomi had to go to court to get her son back. She didn't have a lawyer, but the baby daddy did, and she was a strong one. His lawyers stated that Naomi had seizures and they didn't think she was stable enough to raise him. Naomi told them that she didn't miss any appointments for the parenting class. She went home and got a paper in the mail saying could visit her son, but must pay child support. Naomi felt like she was back to square one. She called her son and checked on him. It was killing her inside because it's hard to let a child go, She didn't let her seizures stop her from raising her kids once again, but she didn't get a chance to see her son before she left again. She was really trying to find a doctor that would help her get off her medication. She heard that CBD oil was good and had a 99% chance of helping the seizures, She was having them in her sleep. The doctor always told her not to stress, but life is sometimes stressful.

Naomi was just taking care of the 4th child, who was 6 years old and who was the only child in her custody then. She didn't have a choice; she had to get up each day and couldn't be depressed because six-year-olds want something to do all the time. Naomi still didn't have her license; she had to wait another year because the doctor was talking about EKG damage on the left side of her brain, She had to stop doing drugs now that she was in her forties, which she accepted. Like when it came to trusting guys, she was learning to do things differently later in her life.

She had to leave the family, which was hard because they say blood is thicker than water, but that's questionable. She could hear God now when she couldn't before. She wanted to succeed in her dreams. Naomi could tell you this: whatever you think God can do, he can. Everything is about time and place.

LONELY AND WITH A DISABILTY

Naomi had to learn that she couldn't tell the jobs she was applying for that she had seizures because they wouldn't hire her. She finally got her own place after her aunt told her and she didn't need to work and that she should stay home and raise the kids. She did, though it was hard with three kids and her grandson.

When Naomi was younger, her family always said she was a rebellious smart ass, but all she was doing was telling the truth about how the family was. What they wouldn't say, Naomi would. But they told her to stay in her place as a child.

Just have trust in God and work on changing your mindset towards life. Rely on yourself; you can only trust anybody on this earth to a certain extent.

Naomi saw this lady in a store and the lady asked her if she could see God. Naomi said no and the lady asked why she would pray to an idol she couldn't see..

Naomi said, "The reason you can't see God is because he lives in you and your body is your temple. It's in how you move, like God would."

Naomi tried not to be a negative person. Everybody went through hard things in life, but if she thought and talked positively, she could train herself to be positive. Naomi always thought she had a problem when the doctor said she couldn't drive, but God still made a way for her and the kids to get around. She also learned not to let anyone speak over her or control her life because that negative person would clap back.

The people that try to abuse your kindness will regret it. It's the little things. For example, listening to or encouraging someone. But because you have this glow about you, you have to be careful with people. If there's a family member or good friend, be careful about what you trust and believe from them. Don't try to sugarcoat it or try to think positively because people are so fake these days. They think they can buy you and you don't have to ask so you think it's okay at first. If you think someone is a good person, it can be confusing. They can have bad intentions. They might be nice to your face, then talk behind your back. But like they say, everything comes to light eventually.

They always say they're on your side, but actions speak louder than words.

Naomi learned that people will fake it until they make it. Also, when Naomi made that move, she needed her license back. That was her goal and she knew she had to finish what she started if she wanted to change. Naomi had to fail in order to see that and to fight for herself and her family. She didn't used to see these things, so she would usually go back and then have to start all over, but this time she was tired.

Naomi met a man that lived in the same apartment complex as her. He came over to fix Naomi's toilet. They began to talk and exchanged phone numbers. Then they started seeing each other, but after the third time, he stopped talking to Naomi and they went their separate ways. They would still bump into each other and say hello, but that was it. Naomi was still struggling to dress well and didn't think she was beautiful. She wondered why that man stopped talking to her. She asked God to remove him from her life if he wasn't for her and he was different after that, But Naomi snapped back and started loving herself. One day, Naomi was sitting outside when he passed her by and then came back. He wanted to talk to her like he was a dog chasing a cat. Naomi had to let go. Like older people always said to her, if someone came back, it meant so much more.

Three months went by, and things were good; there was no drama. But then Naomi had a problem. She needed to go get her grandkids, but she couldn't pass the driving test. Even though she studied and studied, she took it three times and failed. But she started to think that maybe she could go to Florida and just get replacement driver's license. She was thinking of going back, but this new man was also pulling her in a different direction. He was so respectful. She trusted him and felt comfortable around him and she made him feel the same way. It was all naturally falling into place. He had his own place, too, and a car, so he was holding down the fort and being a man. Naomi was not used to that. She was only used to men using her, so this helped her decide to stay. She told herself she would never find another man like that. Naomi told herself she had to take a risk, which she didn't normally do, but she had learned in past relationships she couldn't buy the world or the right man.

You're the only one who can make yourself happy. To stop attracting the same type of people, you must heal the parts of yourself that once needed them. But you can be your own worst critic, afraid instead of realizing that you are gifted.

Naomi began to have more seizures and she felt lost, not sure where to go from there. Her mind was not how it used to be. She still wanted to reach her goals, but she didn't know how. But God still has avenues for you, allowing you to still make your goals happen even if it has to be in a different way from others.

Naomi said, "If you don't see your worth, they won't see it either." Naomi was a fighter. That meant fighting men in her relationships. that was how Naomi was taught to stand up for herself. She had seen a lot of abuse. She had seen men use, beat, and threaten to kill women, telling them, "If I can't have you, no one else will."

Narcissists always move on with no problem because they think you are not strong enough to move on and will come back to them. They will manipulate you and they always say they're never leaving you unless you leave them.

Stop trying to please everybody; that's not balance. Stop trying to be perfect. Stop trying to box yourself in. Stop trying to control everything. Settling is suffering. When you do move to the next level, you have to separate from others so that you can hear God's voice. You are not alone, and we get separated from people because they're the ones who know our wounds, so God wants us to be unrecognizable. Don't mislabel this season. Insecurity is designed to get you to down. Display what God wants to you to display and leave the life of insecurity. Build up walls by healing but build doors too. Take your peace with you.

It can be stormy at the end. A good example is Jonah from the bible. He was rebelling,, then Noah went through the storm for God and was favored.

Naomi was going through this season, getting embarrassed that she was having to travel. But she trusted God to help her move to the other state. She was going by faith during the storm. She was not perfect because she was impatient to drive and work but God told her to sit herself down and listen. She learned that God would allow her to be embarrassed so she could find purpose. She didn't want any man that was not living his purpose and was just watching her because it didn't make sense.

Don't speak of where you are, but where you're going. Don't go off of a person's potential, go off the fruit of their labor.

Naomi learned that beginning in the right direction is better than speeding. Sometimes by slowing down, you will speed up.

There's something unique about a person that grows from their struggles and uses the lessons from their experiences. If you don't care what you did or how many times you fell, you can show others that they can overcome that mountain too.

While Naomi was living in Little Rock, she was living in an apartment. For a whole year, she stayed in the house, not moving the car, either. She felt like she was in prison. She didn't like apartments because of all she went through when she had lived in them. Naomi was not a fan of apartments, except for duplexes. But every bill was paid, even for the car. Still, when she moved into the apartment, she struggled. She was trying to transfer everything from Florida to Little Rock, so she couldn't pay rent her first month. The landlord said to her, "You *just* moved here." She couldn't understand what was going on. Naomi told her she would pay by the end of the month, so they did that and added late fees. But she paid it, so everything was good. The next month, something went wrong. She couldn't pay her rent on time, but the landlord told her she couldn't wait until the end of the month again. Naomi asked if she could pay by the 15th and the landlord agreed. Naomi prayed. She did move there because she trusted God. Naomi said to herself that she showed God what she was due, so she was giving God thanks this time instead of complaining. She filed her income taxes and her money came before the 15th, and she didn't have any more problems with her rent for the rest of the year.

At the end of the year, Naomi was going through it mentally. The pandemic was going on and there was too much racism. Naomi said to herself that this battle was not hers. She was really out of her comfort zone with things not working like she planned. The door kept getting shut on her. But she got a brand -new car. She kept asking God wha she missed. She started feeling down, asking God if she needed to move because she felt like she did when she left before. Once again, she was getting nowhere. Naomi tried to hang in there. She battled her mind, trying to figure it out if she should go back and get t her comfort back. Who wants to struggle if they don't have to? During this time, she was listening to motivational speakers. Sometimes you just have to lift yourself up.

Naomi learned during this time that she had a gift she had always wanted to know about. She helped others so much that she forgot about herself, but now she was learning about herself. She started thinking. She sat down and got to know herself. She guessed this was different than all the times she thought she already knew herself and why she had to go all the way to Little Rock to see God's plans. Naomi realized if she couldn't see anything, she should still trust God.

SECOND CHANCE

Naomi had a second chance in life that she didn't know that she could have. She had been living in this apartment for a year and she was finally stable not just in her living situation, but her mindset. Naomi met a good man the year before. He was amazing, but it didn't feel right because she didn't have a job. She used to pay for everything, and she didn't want him or anybody to think that she was lazy, but it didn't even turn out like that. She had been with him for six months now and she felt so comfortable with him. Naomi had to let go of something; she had to get rid of her old number. He kept asking her why she still had that number. Naomi told her sister that her family would be calling her and not to give out her new number. The next day, a family member called Naomi. Naomi said she was on the right track.

You can turn your past into your strength and it doesn't have to be a crisis. It can be the happiest moment of your life, a moment when you rediscover who you are and what you want. There comes a moment when you realize that you can actually live your dreams and that it's not too late. While Naomi was waiting, she had to encourage herself because she wondered why God sent her a man and not finances. She wanted that first, but God's plans went another direction Then Naomi needed something with the car. She couldn't drive well at first. She was trying to get a job but she went into a depression. Naomi asked God what was going on because she was willing to work now.

Naomi could go to Florida and get her license like that. Every time she made arrangements, something pushed Naomi back, but she figured it out. There's that that old saying, "three strikes and you're out," and Naomi planted that seed. That's why you have to be careful what you say, and your thoughts play a part too. She kept telling herself it could have been worse, so that made her grateful. She wondered what her purpose was. Naomi knew God was preparing her for a house and also her husband, but while waiting, she was getting frustrated that she was telling people that God would bless them, but she was not seeing the same happen for her. Her sister asked Naomi how she could preach and not believe it herself. d Because of that, she tried to go another route. People always looked at her as a Christian she wondered how they saw that when she had done evil things. But always know how good God is and if you don't see God doing good things or if he's allowing bad stuff to happen, don't forget God will be with you through your process. He will make stuff easier on your journey.

Naomi had both people that knew her and people that didn't saying they wished they didn't have to worry or that they wished they could stay home. Hearing this always made Naomi mad because she took it like an insult. If they only knew it was always going to be God's timing. not yours.

Do you remember when you were a kid and you saw an ant hill on the sidewalk and stepped on it or kicked it down? That's us. The ants just rebuild again with no problem. You can rely on your strength and hope to overcome absolutely anything in your life. This also boosts your motivation, your confidence, and your trust in yourself. Without love, success is nothing and has no value. Our personalities are not complete. This part is important; you have to be as precise as a clock. Your love life is going to be paved with changes that are going to deeply influence who you truly are and what you expect from yourself. For you to know how to deal with it and react the right way, you will need to focus on communication. Not only it is a cornerstone of your relationships (and you will see clearly that communication will be a key asset to your progress in your love life), but it will also affect the way you react to others' words. You often replay conversations in your head, thinking of what you should have said or why the other person said what they said to you. You usually put your entire personality into question because of this. You only evolve from what others say, not closing yourself off and giving up. But on the other hand, be sure, certain, and determined. Speak aloud what you've always wanted in your love life. Dig deep inside of yourself without hiding anything to discover what you really expect from your love life, not what others expect from you. Reveal it to yourself. You have all these things you want to say and do, but you have to dare to go for it. Make sure to take advantage of your circumstances to build and live your ideal love life. You have to deal with every single aspect of your love life in order to help you completely get rid of blockage, fears, and any obstacles that might prevent you from having the right relationship. The person you are today is completely influenced by your past and this is especially true for the way you deal with your love life. The relationships you witnessed and the ones you were in with your parents, your friends, and other adults all leave a permanent mark on you and the way you react, the way you express your emotions, and what you expect from relationships. In order to erase every single blockage that stands in your way to pure happiness in your love life, this will be important because past memories and obstacles often prevent you from making better decisions for your love life or expressing what you truly want. It prevents your path towards happiness. Moving on from past issues and memories will definitely erase hard feelings you've been experiencing and help you master your reactions and be surer of what you can and should do. It will help you to improve your love life because you will avoid conflicts and by avoiding overthinking, you avoid jeopardizing your self-esteem. It's also very important to learn how to focus on the future of your love life because having a goal gives you a reason and a purpose. There's no better reward than the satisfaction of building something or the confidence to know that you are actually going somewhere in your love life.

God can heal. For Naomi, he allowed her to heal through books, but it can be different for you: songs, sports, etc. If you are disabled, you have gifts too. Naomi couldn't believe it. For years, she didn't know that, and she kept falling and getting back up. But most of us were never taught to do that or how to hear messages from God, so we continue making the wrong turns. It doesn't have to be that way. Have you ever asked yourself why you are here on this earth? If you aren't sure of this answer or feel you haven't lived up to your potential, please open your mind and heart. It will change the course of your life, but no one can give you permission to fulfill your purpose, it's all up to you.

Naomi spent a lot of her earlier years in pain and suffering, never feeling good enough or appreciated, always seeing the flaws in herself, and wishing she was someone else. Where Naomi was at in her mindset now, she realized fear was a mind killer and everything begins in the mind. We frequently dread labor in our contemporary culture since it is linked with stress, uncertainty, and fatigue. But the job ahead of you doesn't have to be difficult; work can be fluid and powerful as well. We also tend to live in the dark. Many of our days pass us by undetected, and we go to bed wondering what we accomplished that day. Naomi would urge you to beware of the job that has to be completed if you haven't made the necessary preparations for your job, implying that you must meticulously lay out all of your plans before proceeding. It's time to ask yourself some questions: what are you working on at the moment? What tools do you use? Do you have a sense of balance? Are you goal-driven? Are you sure you understand what you're getting yourself into? Is it possible for you to allow yourself to feel powerful and strong, or are such emotions something you'd rather avoid? We don't often allow ourselves to fully appreciate our achievements because we don't have time or we aren't in the mood, but don't let that get in the way of success. We don't even need a significant or life-changing event to be this joyful. We can be this happy all the time. Take responsibility for your own happiness. Just have the courage to shift your attention away from the things that have gone wrong in your life and focus on the positive things that remain because without peace of mind, even the rich man is poor. This is a reminder to check your perspective and make sure you are not creating negative emotions by overthinking. It's okay to feel your emotions, but be careful not to stay stuck in negativity. If something doesn't go your way, achieve harmony and balance in your life. To tackle difficulties with patience and serenity, it takes understanding the conflicting forces inside you. You do not have to be at odds. Make any important choices with caution and know that excellent decisions will lead to positive outcomes for you. Moderation and self-control may help you handle problems in your life by indicating that you have come to an end of a particular cycle in your life. This could be obvious, but in some cases, these cycles can show you what you have learned and what there still is to learn and that it's time for a new cycle to begin, whether it's psychological, emotional, spiritual, or physical. You are moving on to a new chapter and it is time to allow the world to shape itself around you and encourage you to see your unique beauty. Whether or not you fit the modern standard of what is considered beautiful doesn't matter; you are charming and beautiful no matter what you look like on the outside. When you see yourself as beautiful, so will everyone else. Don't get caught up in comparing yourself; instead, try to remember that your energy is what- makes you attractive to the people who are meant to be in your life. Encourage yourself to know your worth. Let life come to you. There are times to take big actions and there are times when what you need is to sit still and stay where you are at. Don't chase after a specific outcome. Things will happen behind the scenes and arrange themselves in your favor. Trust in divine timing. Don't be afraid to go it alone and do things differently.

But Naomi knew that God waited for her.

To Be Continued.

Also Available from J. Kenkade Publishing

ISBN: 978-1-944486-04-4
Visit www.amazon.com
Author: Rahsaan Aki Taylor

A dose of inspiration for every day of your life. Each day, we are faced with challenges that we must conquer and overcome. The contents of this book will help you maintain, stay afloat, and solve some of your troubles. There is a skill, a strategy, and an art to living a prosperous and peaceful life.

Also Available from J. Kenkade Publishing

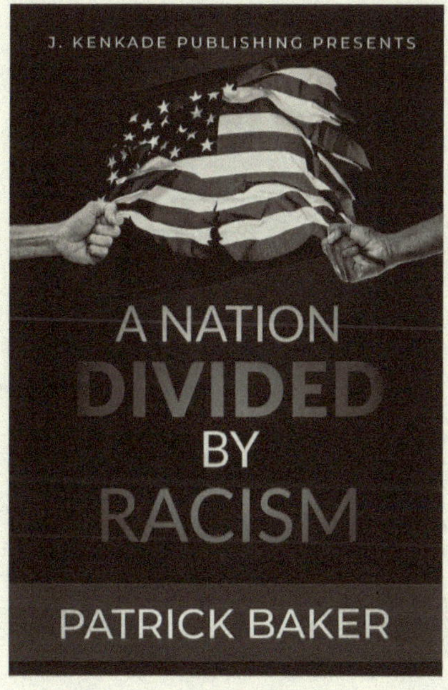

ISBN: 978-1-955186-54-9
Visit www.amazon.com
Author: Patrick Baker

We live in a world where, although we share the world with different people and ethnicities, we live with hate, malice, envy, and strife toward one another. "A Nation Divided by Racism" addresses these matters within an open dialogue.

www.ingramcontent.com/pod-product-compliance
Lightning Source LLC
LaVergne TN
LVHW050943080826
845145LV00004B/1387

* 9 7 8 1 9 5 5 1 8 6 4 7 6 *